Table

MW00915440

My Free Gift To You

If you would like a free workbook, along with a 30 minute video and audio of me personally walking you through the Creativity Checklist please visit:
http://www.creativitychecklist.com/freegift

Once there, please provide a quality email address and I'll send you the workbook and walkthrough video as my way of saying thanks and purchasing this book.

See you over at http://www.creativitychecklist.com/freegift

Tim

How The Creativity Checklist Came To Life

For years I constantly struggled trying to share the ideas in my head with others around me.

I had million-dollar ideas stuck in my head, yet I couldn't seem to share them with anyone on my staff, expensive copywriters or customers.

I was tired, so I bought everything to help me explain my ideas better: copywriting courses, product creation courses, and even expensive personal mentoring from a who's who of internet marketing.

Nothing really seemed to fit or really helped me out.

Until one day while I was out boozing with a buddy of mine...

There, in the middle of a tiny dive bar, a stream of consciousness (ok, maybe drunkenness) hit me. Out of no-where all of these questions starting pouring out of my head, filling up cocktail napkin after cocktail napkin and suddenly I had clarity and confidence in my ability to properly share anything at any time with those around me.

The next morning I woke up and decided to put it to the test.

That's when I trudged down to a local coffee shop (the same one I'm writing this book in) and got to work.

Over the next thirty minutes I simply repeated each question to myself and systematically answered them on paper.

One page turned to three and finally to five pages of notes on a single idea. That had never happened before.

I was so excited that I rushed home, scanned my handwritten notes into the computer and instantly sent them off to my copywriter and staff.

I was so proud of my accomplishment that I announced to my staff that I wanted to launch this new idea in a matter of days, not weeks or months like it normally took.

Then I waited...

Within an hour my copywriter called me on the phone (which he never does):

"Tim, what the hell is this PDF you sent me? Normally I have to pry information out of you and this checklist, or whatever it is, gave me more than enough information to write the letter. I know it normally takes a few days, but with this checklist, I'm going to have the letter to you by tomorrow. I have no idea what you did, but keep doing it."

If only you could have seen my smile – I was grinning ear to ear.

But I'll be honest, even though I hoped I had writer's block crushed once and for all, I knew the proof would be in the numbers.

Emotions might lie; but numbers don't.

Within a week I had the offer up for sales and the sales started to pour in!

In four days I collected close to $10,000 in sales from an idea I had struggled with for MONTHS to get out of my head.

If only I had this checklist years ago, there is no telling how much more money I would have made.

That's why I'm so excited to share it with you, because I know what it's like to stare at a blank page (or worse, an empty bank account) and think, "if only I could actually act on one of these ideas."

If that sounds familiar – welcome; you're in the right place!

Or perhaps you're a successful online marketer who's looking for a way to train your staff, reduce your production time, or increase your bottom line.

Frankly, I don't care what the situation is, because ANYONE can benefit from this checklist!

I do have a word of warning though: do not let the simplicity of the checklist fool you.

You'd be naïve to dismiss it as only a series of questions for you to use occasionally.

In fact, I urge you to do the same thing I did once I discovered the checklist.

#1: Write the questions on a 3x5 card (or in your smart phone) and carry it wherever you go

#2: Next time you have an idea, pull out the checklist and get to work

There's that dreaded W word.

I'm sorry to disappoint any biz op seekers or wanna-be push button millionaires – you're going to have to invest a little more time and brain power to see the full benefit of this checklist.

But then again – if you could spend 30 minutes and make $10,000 how many times would you do it?

That's what I thought.

With that in mind, let's get to work!

Why Use The Creativity Checklist?

If you've ever struggled with communicating your thoughts or ideas to someone else, this is the checklist for you!

With it you'll finally be able to explain exactly what it is you want with your product or service to anyone you desire. You can finally share problems you want to overcome, how it's going to happen, competitors you need to be aware of, and how to build the best product possible.

I use it with my staff, outsourcers, design team, copywriters and even our tech staff.

With it I'm able to explain every step, concept and exactly how I want things done.

In the past, I use to come up with an idea, gather my staff and stumble around for HOURS trying to extract the idea from the dark corners of my mind.

It was even worse with my copywriter. I'd hire a guy for thousands of dollars only to draw a blank stare once he asked me about the product itself.

I used the same "Ummmm... I don't know but I'll tell you later," more times than I care to remember.

I can't tell you how many times I woke up the morning of a product launch or training with white knuckle fear because I didn't believe in my ability to deliver on what I had already promised – simply because I didn't believe in my ability to properly explain the idea or concept in my head.

Several times I thought about canceling them and refunding the money while I hid in the corner because I had tricked myself again into thinking I had the ability to share my ideas with the world.

But no more.

Now, each step of the checklist gives me a new level of clarity, understanding and confidence.

Remember the $10,000 idea I referenced in the last chapter? Here is what you didn't know.

Before that checklist I had that idea stuck in my brain for MONTHS. Six months to be exact.

Imagine having a $10,000 check hanging over your head for months and you being unable to connect the dots enough to cash it.

Talk about frustrating and annoying!

Let's get into the actual checklist and how it's going to help you.

What Is The Creativity Checklist?

The creativity checklist is an 11 step system for you to use with any product, service or idea you have now or in the future.

Here are the questions to ask yourself with the checklist:

1. What problem does your product/service solve?

2. What proof do you have that it works?

3. What will be included with your product/service?

4. What is your story behind the product/service?

5. How recent or believable is your product or service?

6. What are the features/benefits of using your product or service?

7. What are your competitors for this product or service?

8. What other income possibilities - recurring or one time only - can I have in addition to this product or service?

9. What are the hooks/angles we can take with this product/service?

10. What testimonials or third party data do you have about your product or service?

11. How much time and/or money did it take you to develop your product or service?

Now that you've seen the checklist in its entirety, let's look at each question in detail.

Question #1

What problem does your product/service solve?

If you think about it, people only buy solutions to their problems.

If they're fat they're not joining a gym because of its location or because it has a yoga class. They're buying a gym membership because they want to be healthier and ultimately lose weight.

Problem: Fat

Solution: Gym → Skinny

Now, you could totally use stuff like your location, on-site day care, and 24 hour access to solve additional problems (close to your house, keep the kids busy while you exercise and workout on your schedule), but NEVER attempt to sell something that doesn't solve someone's problem.

For instance, as I write this, I'm listening to Spotify with my noise cancelling headphones. I bought Spotify so could have music wherever I wanted it (problem) and the headphones to drown out all the wannabe authors around me (another problem).

Still need some convincing? Ok let's talk about you for a second. Ask yourself this question:

Why did I buy this creativity checklist?

Chances are something you saw on the sales page made you identify a problem you are currently having (writer's block, information overload, and being overwhelmed), and you are using this checklist to solve that problem.

Honestly, if you can't list at least three different problems your product or service solves, you might want to rest on that idea and go on to another one.

The more problems your product or service solves, the more chances you have to make a sale.

Don't think your product or service solves that many problems? I suggest you spend at least 20 minutes away from the computer and distractions writing out this checklist.

Question #2

What proof do you have that it works?

In today's society customers (and potential customers) are more skeptical than ever. They've been burned, abused, kicked and spit out from so many businesses that they have their guard up at all times.

Just think about all the software and services out there that exist solely to block advertiscments, TV commercials, and other forms of advertisement.

And in this economy, with the consumer's dollar having to be stretched further than ever, you have to go ABOVE and beyond to prove your case to the consumer.

The way you do that (and get them to trust you in the process) is through proof.

Think back to where you bought this product.

I didn't just say here's my checklist; now give me your money, did I?

Of course not, instead, I explained how I came up with the checklist and I showed concrete proof that it worked with evidence from a recent successful campaign.

Why did I do that? I mean, I've sold over a million dollars' worth of products online, so why didn't I just rest on my past accomplishments to sell this book to you?

Because it doesn't matter what people's past perception of you is; all that matters is here and now and what have you done lately.

There are several smart ways to showcase proof.

- Screenshots

- Before vs. after photos

- Testimonials (we'll talk about this in a few)

- Third party data (also coming shortly)

- Demonstrations (this works well with software/plugins)

At the end of the day, a consumer wants a solution to their problem. By showing them several ways they can be successful and your past accomplishments under similar circumstances, you gain their trust.

The more proof you can pile on the better. Honestly, I don't think you could ever OVER DO proof when it comes to selling a product or service.

I'll share a critical tip when it comes to using the proper proof later (under the recent and believable section), so be on the lookout for it.

Question #3

What will be included with your product/service?

This is where you start to lay out the different services or modules you're going to include in with your product or service.

If you're stuck trying to figure that out, here's a simple solution I call my 5x5 method.

Take whatever the problem you're trying to solve and break it down to 5 major parts.

Once you do that, take each major part and break it down into 5 minor parts.

When you've done that, simply bullet point each major and minor part and you've got a complete outline of your product or service.

As you work through the rest of the questions, don't be surprised if more ideas on what to include or take out occur. Simply note them and keep moving forward.

Oh and here's a tactic I've used recently...

I put out a 3 hour long training called the tripwire training (http://tripwiretraining.com) that showed people how to create information products just like this one. At the end of it I asked for feedback and testimonials.

When I did, I got 99% positive feedback and a few people who wanted me to expand on certain areas of the training.

So what did I do? I simply shot additional content and released it for free to the buyers.

Think about that for a second.

Imagine buying a product and then a week later being told - hey, you know what - I wanted to send you additional content for free.

Then a week later they get another email saying the same thing with some more free content.

Do you think that if you did that you'd get people to know, like and trust you much faster?

Of course you would.

Look, I am not saying you should release a half completed product (you shouldn't). The bottom line is you can never cover everything (no matter how long you take or have to present the material). You should use the follow-up process to enhance the customer experience and stand out from your peers.

Question #4

What is your story behind the product/service?

People learn better from stories than from just plain Jane facts.

Think back to the beginning of this book - do you remember the story I told you about me scrawling out all of these questions in a dive bar on a cocktail napkin?

Now let me ask you this – if you close your eyes can you imagine what that picture looks like?

Chances are you can and that is because of the story I told you about the creation of this checklist.

The good news is EVERY product or service has a similar story just waiting to be shared with the world.

If you think about it long enough, the story will come.

Also go back and read the beginning of this book.

Notice how I talked about my struggle before and my results after using the checklist.

That wasn't by chance.

In fact, it was deliberate because:

1. It is a true story.

2. It shows that I was able to overcome a problem using the same product I sold you.

Remember back to question 1- people only buy solutions to their problems. Here's another secret - people are pussies.

Sorry for the strong language, but it's true.

We don't like to fail, we don't want to look bad, and worst of all we don't want to have to admit to someone else we were wrong.

By sharing your story of struggle and overcoming obstacles, people can't help but put themselves in your shoes and imagine themselves doing the same.

Think about people like Tony Robbins (he lived in a one bedroom apartment washing dishes in the tub) and Frank Kern (he was sued by the FTC and lost everything) or any other motivational speaker or presenter.

They all have that defining moment when everything changed for the better.

The more you can show your struggle and then your triumph, the more people will relate and buy into your product or service.

Question #5

How recent or believable is your product or service?

Life is a lot like the Janet Jackson song "What Have You Done for Me Lately?"

Customers, affiliates, co-workers, bosses, really anyone involved in any type of relationship with another person operates by this rule.

Don't believe me? Ok, stop telling your spouse that you love them or stop doing something you normally do and see how long things remain the same.

In fact, just stop showing up to work and let me know how long it takes for someone else to notice.

Like it or not, we are a results based society where our success and self-worth are dictated by our latest accomplishments, not the furthest ones.

Almost 10 years ago I was trapped on an Air Force base for 7 days during an ice storm.

Things got so bad and we had the only backup generator on base, so for those 7 days I stood watch and helped feed over 6,000 people three times a day. At the end of it I got a commendation medal and few extra days leave.

Now let me ask you something - when you were reading that short (but true) story, did you start saying, who cares, what does this have to do with anything, or just get on with it already?

See, it happens to us all.

You must do everything within your power to show that your product or service is successful in today's market not last month's and certainly not last year's because customers want to know what you're offering them works under present conditions – not the past

Take this book, for instance – as soon as I got a positive result, I decided to share it with the world.

Why?

Because a $10,000 windfall looks amazing if it happened within 30 days of releasing this book, but not so amazing a year from now.

The other thing you need to be concerned about is believability.

You can actually do more HARM than good if you're offer seems too good to be true.

Imagine hiring a fitness coach to help you run better.

You interview two of them, and the first guy tells you that by this time next week he'll have you in good enough shape to run a 26 mile marathon.

Guy number two says that by this time next week you'll be able to run around the block without stopping or being out of breath.

Which one do you believe?

Of course you're going to believe the second guy! Even if the first guy could actually deliver on his promise, so many people wouldn't believe him because they think it's too good to be true.

If you're going to make a claim that seems almost too good to be true, I suggest you have a ton of PROOF and address their skepticism head-on or be prepared to be ignored and labeled as a hype master.

Question #6

What are the features/benefits of using your product or service?

Do you know the difference between a feature and a benefit?

A feature is something your product or service does; a benefit is the result of that product or service.

For example, this toaster comes in 4 different colors (feature) SO you can match it to your existing home decor (benefit).

You'll notice I capitalized the word SO in that sentence and I did so for a specific reason.

If you've ever struggled to come up with a list of features or benefits for your product or service, simply list out what your product/service does and the results that are accomplished when doing so. Then connect the two with the word so.

Here's another example to make sure you get it. This creativity checklist is 11 questions that allow you to properly think out any idea you have (feature) SO that you can eliminate writer's block, overcome being overwhelmed, and finally get all those million dollar ideas out of your head and onto paper (benefit).

Your goal with this question is to list out as many features and benefits that your product or service offers. The more features and benefits you can think of allows your copywriter (or you) to target different markets with different messages.

Using this book as an example, I originally created the checklist to solely use with ideas that I wanted to turn into standard information products. It was only once I started looking at the features and benefits that I was able to see how helpful the same checklist would be for software creators, service providers, and non-fiction authors.

Because I am able to target several different niches (or end users), I am now able to cast a much wider net searching for customers. I bet once you start writing down your product's features and benefits, new target markets will rapidly appear out of thin air.

Question #7

Who are your competitors for this product or service?

I'll be honest, I slack when it comes to this section, and I bet that has cost me thousands of dollars in the process. With that being said, here is what I would do with this section.

First you need to understand that there is nothing new under the sun and most "new" ideas are just a twist or a combination of old ideas. Once you understand that, you'll be able let go of the limiting belief that everything must be brand new to be successful.

The fact that most ideas are old ideas will also make your research ability MUCH easier. Instead of creating out of thin air, you can simply find an old product or service and improve upon it (that's my favorite method, by the way).

By looking at, and in some cases purchasing, your competitor's products, it will give you an insider's view of what they're doing right and places in which you can excel. For instance, I once saw a listing of outsourcers that was priced ridiculously low and the product itself was over 300 pages, but the numbers didn't lie - it had sold over 5,000 copies in less than a year.

So I took that original idea, and used the same information in specific markets (Facebook, Kindle, etc.) and then added more items to the sales funnel. The result was that we sold fewer copies than the original, but the complete funnel had been responsible for over $60,000 in income this year alone.

I would have never gotten the idea without looking at what my competition was already doing. You can also use this section to reference certain websites, books, courses, etc. The more you can contain the "chaos" of researching into an easy-to-manage-and-understand cheat sheet, the better.

Question #8

What other income possibilities, recurring or one time, can I have in addition to this product or service?

You remember the example I just shared above about the outsourcing report? Despite selling over 5,000 copies of their report, they offered me NOTHING else after the sale. With this type of report, the information inside of it becomes stale in less than 2 months, which means I would NEED a new copy of the report every two months (at least).

Yet they didn't offer it to me. So I created my own. On the back of my outsourcing report I offered a low ticket micro continuity offer that resulted in thousands of dollars a month in recurring income for doing the same work I was already doing.

I also added a case study to the sales funnel and before you knew it I had the single largest launch in that specific niche in a year.

That's the power of this question.

As a product or service provider you should always be asking what's next. You should always be looking for things that can help automate, simplify or scale someone's business. Software, personal coaching, group coaching, and done for you services are just a few examples of things that could and should be offered.

If you can add something to your sales funnel that allows recurring income to happen, do it. I can't think of any recurring possibilities with this book, but depending on where you purchased this from, you might have been taken to a One Time Offer for a tripwire training that you can see here: http://www.tripwiretraining.com.

This training is over 3 hours of pure content on putting this checklist to use to create small information products that lead to bigger profits. It is the logical "next step" to this book and also gives me the ability to sell this book for so little, because the real profits come from the backend (or funnel, as it's sometimes called).

Don't worry if you can't create your own products or services. If you approach someone who has an existing product or service you already use and enjoy, chances are you can show them the benefit to have it included in your sales funnel as an affiliate.

I love being an affiliate because I usually get paid 50% of the product price without having to do anything. Talk about easy money!

In fact, I'd recommend you picking up the tripwire training and seeing how you can create small products to put in front of affiliate products you'd like to promote.

Recently, I did this for a large internet marketer and it resulted in a $50,000 payday.

Question #9

What are the hooks/angles we can take with this product/service?

If you think back to question six, where I talked about features and benefits, I talk about casting as wide as a net as possible to search for new customers. This question will help you flush out that idea even further.

The way I like to look at this question is how many different ways I can sell the same thing to different customers. The more fish hooks you put into the water, the better your chances of catching one.

Here are a couple of examples:

"A ten minute experiment leads to a $10,000 payday" would be a hook or angle I would use with internet marketers looking to for a quick way to turn their ideas into cash.

"Instantly End Overwhelm" is another way I could target internet marketers or really anyone who has felt overwhelmed with ideas.

"Finally Solve Writer's Block" would be something I could share with struggling writers (and product creators) as a hook or angle to get them interested in what I have to say.

The more you can align your message to the right market, the better your chances of success.

The more markets you can be successful in attracting new customers means you have a better chance of selling more products or services.

This question also gives you a chance to show how your product or service stands out from everyone else in your market.

The best part of this is that the product remains the same in each market and it's only the marketing hook or angle that I take which changes.

That means I can create something once and slant it to different markets and get paid forever.

For instance, the general title of this book is *The Creativity Checklist*. But if I add the words *Non-fiction Writers* in front of the original name, I have a brand new product and target market to offer it to.

The same goes for adding the words "Product Creators" in front of the original name - again a new product and a new market without having to change anything but the cover.

Are you starting to see the possibilities here? I sure hope so because with the right hook or angle the possibilities are endless.

Question #10

What testimonials or third party data do you have about your product or service?

Think back to the section on proof. The bottom line is you can NEVER have enough of it and testimonials or third party data are great examples.

Before I talk about those two things, let me share with you what I believe are the only three ways you can sell your product or service.

First, you tell everyone how awesome it is. You can totally do this and you can totally look like a douche doing so. No one likes the guy who brags constantly about how awesome he is. Sure, a few people might listen, but more will be turned off by this "look at me" attitude and message.

Second, you could get other people can tell everyone how awesome you are! Have you ever had a friend who was a vegan or did Crossfit? Chances are if you do, they won't shut up about it. In fact, the joke is this - if you're a vegan who does Crossfit, how do you decide which one to annoy your friends and family with first?

In all seriousness, when you can get others talking about how awesome your product or service is, you've hit pay dirt. Plus, in this economy with limited dollars to spend, customers are looking for sure things more than guessing on their own.

But it goes deeper than that. At the end of the day the end user wants to feel smarter for choosing your product or service and above all they don't want to feel like they made a mistake.

That's why testimonials are so important. They are another symbol to the customer that it's ok to trust you because they trusted you first and got some amazing results. The more you can have your testimonials match your target market the better.

For example, if I was selling this book strictly to authors, I'd want testimonials from other authors talking about how amazing this book is.

Like attracts like.

It's my opinion that you can't overdue testimonials, and the more you use the better. You let others state your case for you. You should actively and aggressively collect them. One way I like to collect them is by using "ethical bribes" on my customers.

For instance, if you would be so kind to go to http://www.creativitychecklist.com/survey and tell me your honest thoughts about this book, I'll be more than happy to send you a free 30 minute video walking you through the creativity checklist along with a worksheet you can use to create and fill out your own checklist.

Don't worry if you've never done one of these before - all I'm looking for is an answer to the following question:

"In your opinion and own words, do you think the creativity checklist will be able to save you time, money, and energy when creating your next product or service? What do you think was the best part of this book? Was it the step-by-step instructions, understanding how to use it on your own business, or finally being able to get all of those ideas out of your head and onto paper?"

See, it's that easy to start asking for and collecting testimonials from your customers. Simply come up with something they'd love to have (that complements your product) and offer it to them in exchange for their honest opinion.

And for those of you scared about asking for their opinion, I'd remind you of two things.

1. If you get a negative review, you can use it as a chance to learn or improve your product or service.

2. If people are asking something of you, especially when it's free, do you think they're going to be negative or rude about it? If they are, simply flush them from your life like soiled toilet paper. They aren't worth the headspace or aggravation of keeping them around.

The third way of providing proof is third party data. This could be government reports, websites, celebrities, etc.

Think of it as a neutral party who is saying something that backs up a claim you're trying to make.

For instance, I could tell you that this is the greatest book ever written about creativity. Some of you might believe me.

Then I could have a few testimonials from people who bought it saying the same thing. More of you would believe them.

But if a big celebrity, like Tim Ferriss or Oprah, came out and said I think creativity is the most important skill you could learn as an entrepreneur, I could use that as third party to back up my claim that you need to own this book.

The best part about third party data it that it is neutral and because of that no one can claim that you faked it or made it up.

I typically like to use third party data in support of an argument that I'm trying to convince of you of.

For instance, if I said you need to write erotica, you might think about it; but if I said, "According to *Writer's Digest*, erotica makes up $3.2 billion dollars of the publishing industry," they sell the reason you need to be writing erotica for me.

By the way, thanks to lawyers, I should remind you that all the examples in this section are just made up and no one actually said, endorsed, or promoted anything of mine. Hug a lawyer today; they need it.

Above all do everything in your power to ensure the information you use with third party data is up to date, and when in doubt, site your sources in your sales materials or products.

Question 11

How much time and/or money did it take you to develop your product or service?

I know it's been awhile, but think back to the beginning of this book and the story I shared with you. Remember when I talked about all the products I bought, the mentoring I took, and the money I spent trying to create this checklist on my own?

I did that for a specific reason.

That story and these questions allowed me to paint a picture for someone who is thinking about doing this process on their own and without this checklist. Think about it - we all know people who have attempted to save some time or money by moving themselves or changing their own oil or brakes.

How many times has that same person come back and talked about what a nightmare that decision was? I'm betting more than once.

Here is where you lay out EVERYTHING you've done to get you to where you are today.

Did it take you 5 years to create your product or service? Write that down. Did it cost you $10,000 and you had to travel all over the world? Write it down. Did you have to travel to a village in India, risk death and dismemberment, get malaria, and then spend your last dollar on a 200 mile train ride (with no AC, of course) to meet with a guru at the end of a 20 mile uphill walk?

No matter how trivial it may seem, write it down. The whole point with this section is to show people how smart they are to have taken the path you're suggesting compared to the one that they go it alone.

The truth of the matter is you could create this checklist on your own. You could read the books, study the courses, hire the coaches, and work on it for the 5 years it took me, OR you could pay a small fee and eliminate the learning curve and get an instant injection of my brain into yours.

The thing to remember is human nature. As humans we are always looking for a shortcut, a hack, a quicker, faster, better way of doing this. Your job is to show them how your product or service does that. No matter what time, no matter what the situation, human nature will prevail.

Just look at the diet industry. So many people are trying to accomplish the same thing - to get you to eat less and work out more. There are pills, potions, and numerous workout contraptions and fad diets that promise to do the same thing but save you time, money, and energy in the process.

So there you have it, the 11 questions I ask myself every time I'm trying to flush out a new product or service. In the next section I'll show you exactly how I use the creativity checklist.

How To Use The Creativity Checklist

I'll admit at times I feel like an analog guy in a digital word. Despite typing this report on a Chromebook while listening to Spotify, I usually resort to the old fashioned pen and paper when it comes to filling out the checklist.

Here's exactly what I do. I write the questions on a 3x5 card or in a text message to myself on my smart phone. Then I grab a yellow legal pad and a Pilot G2 pen and head to my local coffee shop.

Once I'm there I sit at a table, put my headphones in, queue up a specific playlist that plays the same songs over and over and get to work. I find creativity comes when I get away from the computer and all its distractions.

I put my phone on airplane mode and start writing the questions and my answers to them long hand. When I'm done, I go home and scan those notes into a PDF and send them to my staff. If it is a product or service I am looking to outsource, I will put on my Logitech G930 headset and record a screen capture video walking through the checklist for my outsourcers or copywriters.

I record the video using a program called Camtasia or Screencast-O-Matic. When it's finished, I upload the video to YouTube and email a link to my team along with a copy of my checklist. I make the video unlisted on YouTube so no one sees it but the people who have a direct link.

If I need to create a product off the checklist, I use each question to create a new node in a mind map program called Xmind. If I need to do a visual presentation, I'll typically use Powerpoint and create slides from each question of the checklist along with any supporting information. From there I will usually record a screen capture video walking through the product. A lot of the time, I'll pay to have transcripts made of the video to include alongside of it.

For the creativity checklist, here was my process:

Step 1. Use the checklist and all 11 questions to flush out the book

Step 2. Record a screen capture video for my copywriter to create the product sales letter

Step 3. Make a Mindmap using Xmind of the 11 questions

Step 4. Record a 30 minute video walking through the mind map

Step 5. Sit down at the computer and write the actual book

By the time I'm on step 5, I am almost like a machine. As of now I've spent 3 hours writing this book and it is currently 6433 words (and counting). In fact, I wrote all of this in a single sitting using only the mind map as my outline. Because of all the work I did prior to sitting down to write, when it came time to put my thoughts into a Google Doc, the words just flowed like water.

Now remember, this is my process but I don't expect it to be yours.

Honestly, I toyed with the idea of hiring a writer to outsource the actual writing portion of the report based on the video, but their rough draft stunk, so I said screw it and got to work writing it myself. I'm glad I did because as I'm typing these words, I feel a connection to this checklist and the entire creative process that wouldn't be possible if I had someone else writing it.

The bottom line is this - I don't care how you use the checklist, just use it. I don't always use the questions in the order they are written above. If I have the urge to write about the story or proof before anything else, I act on it. If I know exactly what I want included with the product or service, I start there.

This is your world, you design it how it best suits you. And don't be afraid to add, subtract, or combine questions as you see fit. There is no right or wrong way to do it. For years I used other people's checklists and guidelines and they just never felt "right." It wasn't until a drunken night with a buddy that inspiration finally hit me. Give it time and it will come visit you as well, and you'll find the best combination of putting the checklist to use for yourself.

If you're just getting started, my suggestion is to use the checklist exactly how I designed it at first. If at the end of it you don't like it, make a change. But only do that once you've given an honest and real effort to use the checklist as it is now.

The other thing I recommend is setting a timer or a specific deadline to get the checklist finished. Without a deadline, someday turns into never, tomorrow turns into next week and before you know it the idea you thought was amazing is simply forgotten.

Don't let that happen to you.

In fact, here's what I want you to do.

Now that we're close to the end of this book, I want you to grab a piece of paper and spend at least 30 minutes writing down all the ideas you have racing around in your head currently. You don't need to do the checklist for each one; this is just the idea generation phase.

When you're done, I want you to look at each idea and ask yourself some questions about each one.

As yourself, on a scale of 1 to 10, how much would you enjoy working on this project? Take this book for example. I stopped writing last night at 10:45 p.m. and here I am the next morning finishing it up - but I've got a smile from ear to ear and I'm actually enjoying sharing this information with you and the world because I enjoy it! I am more than willing to work on it and the time and energy to do so appear seemingly out of nowhere.

The next question you need to ask yourself is, on a scale of 1 to 10, how much value is this going to bring? Can I be honest? Books typically bring me very little financial value (at the moment), but they serve as great tools to get in front of new potential customers (like you). So this book has little financial value, but it can be valuable if it attracts new people to my business.

It's also the reason why I taught this same checklist in a live class first, then a standalone information product, and finally a book. I did things in the order that they brought value to me and my clients.

If the idea you have seems enjoyable to you but of little value to others, you should probably move on to another idea. Value is seen in the eyes of the consumer and it doesn't matter how much you think everyone NEEDS to have your product or service; it only matters if customers feel the same way.

Once you ask yourself those two questions for each idea, tally up the total score. Ideas that score 15 or less get put away for another day. Only work on ideas that score 16 or higher, and the higher the better. There is only one exception to this rule. If, while going through your idea list, your gut tells you to act on a certain idea, trust it.

It's like this book, so far I've got just a couple of hours into the writing of it. It may be a success or it may be a complete flop, but I don't care because my gut told me to sit down and spend a few hours working on it. Worst case is I publish it and it flops, but at that point I'll only be out a few hours of my time and a few dollars.

I've wasted more time and money doing things of no value, so I feel that this is a better trade off of my time and energy than playing video games or watching Netflix.

Once you have that one idea you want to work on, pull out the checklist and get to work. Spend at least 30 minutes working away from the computer, filling out the checklist. If after that 30 minutes you need more time, take it. I will typically spend thirty minutes to two hours on each checklist. I've also walked away from a checklist during the day, only to find an additional thought or idea strike me during the day that I want to add to it.

If, however, after 30 minutes you find yourself with a blank page, you have two choices. You could keep going with the checklist and try and grind the information out of your brain and onto the page. Or you can simply pick a different idea and start the process over.

I would suggest at first you pick the "low hanging fruit" ideas that easily and quickly come to you and spill them out on the checklist. By doing so you'll get comfortable with the checklist and the process of using it. And don't worry; you can always go back to that other idea anytime you want.

My office is filled with half completed checklists, all waiting on inspiration or explanation to be completed. I've also thrown away a ton of ideas that, after filling out the checklist, I realized weren't as amazing as I once thought. My rule of thumb is if I can't properly explain it to myself in a way to get excited, I scrap it. Life is too short to force bad or incomplete ideas into good ones.

One last thing to consider - how much do you love your idea? I'm fortunate enough to know some pretty big bands in the music business and one of their favorite things to talk about is their hit song and how much they hate and despise playing it now. Think about it; if you're famous for a single song, you almost have to play it at every show, on a radio spot, on TV, and so on. I don't care who you are, if you have to do the same thing a million times over and over, you're going to grow to hate it.

Don't build products or services that you'll grow to hate or despise. Trust me. There is nothing worse than building a successful business around something you can't stand. The checklist can serve as a proving ground to you about much you really want to pursue something.

Wrapping Things Up

Now you have everything. You have the 11 point checklist I use in my business to help get ideas out of my head and into the world. You have my exact process for getting away from the computer and into creative hippie mode (as I call it). Finally, you know the questions I ask myself when evaluating an idea and how I decide if something is worth pursuing or passing on.

There is one last thing I want to remind you of - don't let the simplicity of this checklist or my process fool you. Despite selling over seven figures of products online, before this checklist I was constantly struggling and delayed taking action as a result. Without it, I was fumbling over ideas, missing deadlines, and leaving a ton of money on the table.

I shudder to think back to those painful times. The good news is you don't have to experience any of that. When you put the checklist to use, you'll find writer's block, information overload, and frustration diminish or disappear. All you need to do is sit down and put the checklist to work in your life and business.

If along the way you have a question, comment, or concern, I would welcome them all (plus knowing how this checklist helped you) via email. You can reach me at contacttimcastleman@gmail.com.

Until we see each other again, I wish you good luck producing as much value and enjoyment into the world as possible. With this checklist, anything is a possible.

Tim Castleman

Don't Forget Your Free Gift

If you would like a free workbook, along with a 30 minute video and audio of me personally walking you through the Creativity Checklist please visit:
http://www.creativitychecklist.com/freegift

Once there, please provide a quality email address and I'll send you the workbook and walkthrough video as my way of saying thanks and purchasing this book.

See you over at http://www.creativitychecklist.com/freegift

Tim

Request For Review

Now that you've finished the creativity checklist, would you take just a few seconds out of your day and share your thoughts about it here:
http://www.timreallylikes.com/ccreview

By leaving a review showing others how this book can help them as well.

If you've never written a review - don't worry here an example of one I've recently received to help you:

Review Example:

I found it extremely helpful. It sparked a ton of ideas. It not only helped me be figure out what should go in the product and how my product could help people, it also made me realize that there are other related products I could easily create that will appeal to the same audience. Just working through the steps clarified how I could best organize the material for my students.

And finally, seeing all the pieces laid out in black and white made me really excited about starting to work on the materials.

Overall, it was awesome, and I'll be using it not just on future products, but also for non-fiction books and as a guide for revamping one of my blogs.

Regards,

Bonnie

You can leave your review here:
http://www.timreallylikes.com/ccreview

Once you leave a review be sure to email me at contacttimcastleman@gmail.com and I will send you a special thank you for leaving one.

Made in the USA
San Bernardino, CA
14 June 2020